W9-ANX-468

Watch It Grow
Bee
Barrie Watts

Smart Apple Media

First published in 2004 by Franklin Watts
96 Leonard Street, London EC2A 4XD, United Kingdom
Franklin Watts Australia, 45-51 Huntley Street, Alexandria, NSW 2015
Copyright © 2004 Barrie Watts

Editor: Kate Newport, Art director: Jonathan Hair,
Photographer: Barrie Watts, Illustrator: David Burroughs

Published in the United States by Smart Apple Media
2140 Howard Drive West, North Mankato, Minnesota 56003

Library of Congress Control Number: 2004101771

ISBN 1-58340-502-X

2 4 6 8 9 7 5 3 1

How to use this book

Watch It Grow has been specially designed to cater to a range of reading and learning abilities. Initially children may just follow the pictures. Ask them to describe in their own words what they see. Other children will enjoy reading the single sentence in large type in conjunction with the pictures. This single sentence is then expanded in the main text. More adept readers will be able to follow the text and pictures by themselves through to the conclusion of the bee's life cycle.

Contents

Here is a honeybee. 4

The queen bee lays eggs. 6

The egg is small. 8

The egg hatches. 10

The worker bees feed the larvae. 12

The larva grows. 14

The workers seal the cell. 16

The larva turns into a pupa. 18

The bee emerges. 20

The bee leaves the hive. 22

The bee finds food. 24

The bee stores the food. 26

The workers feed the queen. 29

Word bank 30

Life cycle 31

Index 32

Here is a honeybee.

A honeybee is an insect. This means that it has six legs, a pair of wings, and two eyes. Bees live together in large groups called colonies.

People often keep bees in beehives to collect the **honey** they make. There can be as many as 50,000 bees living in a **hive**. In the wild, bees usually make their homes in hollow trees.

The queen bee lays eggs.

Each colony of bees has a **queen bee**. She is the only bee that can lay eggs. She lays each egg in a different **cell** of the wax **honeycomb** that makes up the **hive**.

The other bees in the hive fall into two groups: female workers and male **drones**. The **worker bees** make the honeycomb wax. It comes from four **glands** under their stomach.

The egg is small.

The bee egg is very small—about as long as a pinhead. The **queen bee** lays most of her eggs when the weather is warm. She lays up to 3,000 eggs each day.

She carefully attaches each egg to the bottom of a **cell**. As soon as it is laid, the egg starts to change. Inside, a bee **larva** is growing.

The egg hatches.

After three days, the egg hatches and a bee **larva** crawls into its **cell**. The larva is creamy-white and about as long as a grain of rice.

The **worker bees** start feeding it a liquid food called **royal jelly**. When the larva is small, it floats in the cell on a pool of royal jelly. Larvae hatch at different times, so they are all different sizes in the cells.

The worker bees feed the larvae.

Younger **worker bees**, called **house bees**, look after the **hive**. They take care of the queen and her eggs and feed the **larvae**.

There can be as many as 10,000 larvae growing in a large hive. The house bees must keep the larvae well-fed, because new bees are needed to work in the hive.

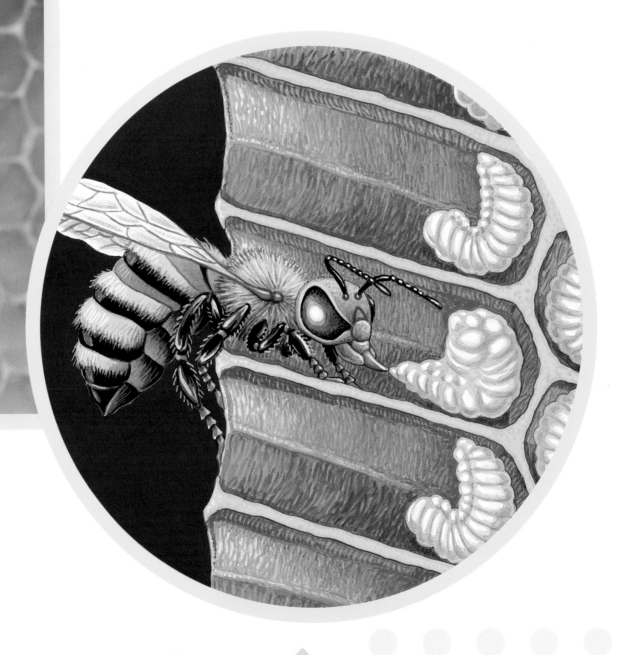

The larva grows.

After three days, the **worker bees** stop feeding **royal jelly** to the **larva**. Instead, they feed the larva **pollen** and **honey**.

The workers look after the larva carefully and feed it more than 1,000 times a day. As the larva grows, it sheds its skin, just like a butterfly caterpillar. It does this five times during its life as a larva.

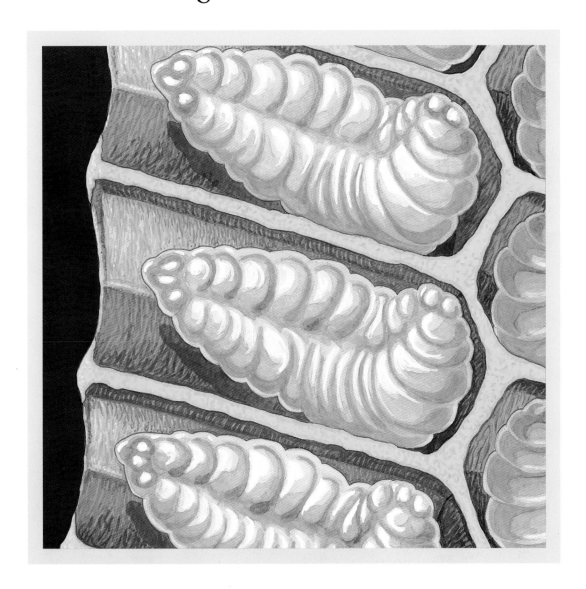

The workers seal the cell.

Eight days after hatching, the **larva** is fully grown and fills the **cell**. It is now so big it cannot curl up. Its mouth is facing the cell entrance.

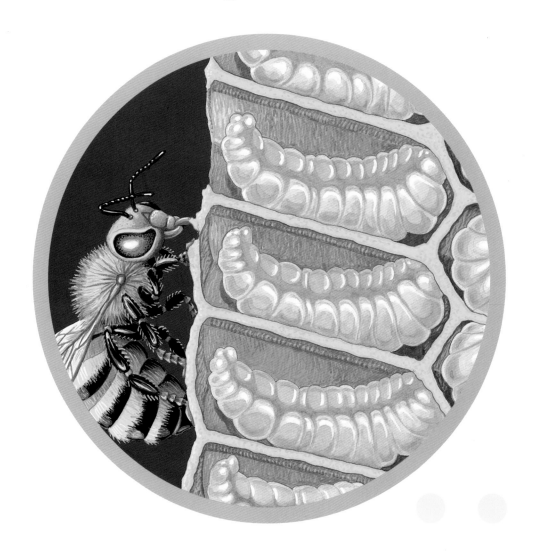

The workers stop feeding the larva and put a cap of wax on the cell to seal it. The cap lets air through so the larva can breathe.

The larva turns into a pupa.

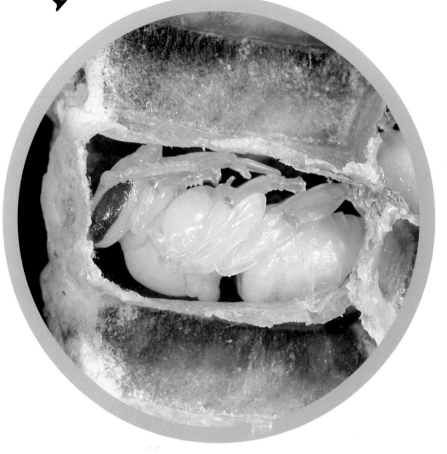

The **larva** cannot feed anymore, and it starts to change into a **pupa**. Three days after the **cell** has been capped, the larva sheds its skin for the last time.

Underneath is a pupa. It looks like a bee without wings. But beneath its soft skin, the pupa is changing into a fully grown bee.

The bee emerges.

After nine days, the **pupa** changes color. It has turned into an adult bee inside the pupa case. Its eyes are dark, and it has grown wings.

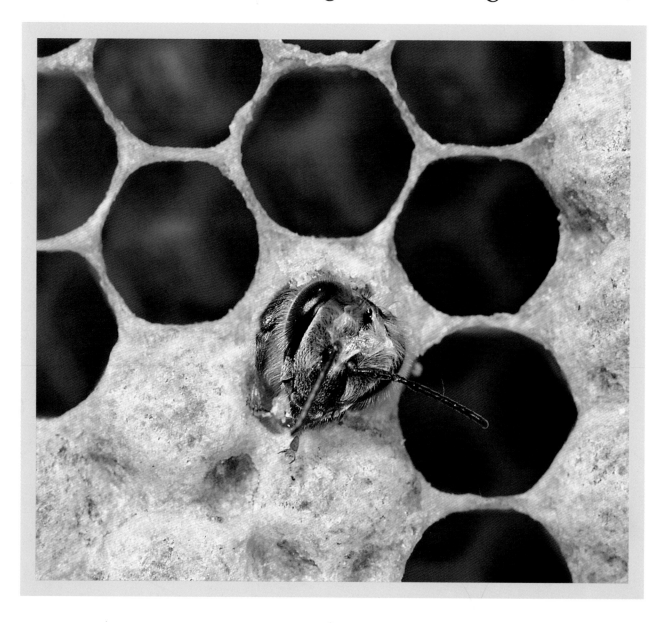

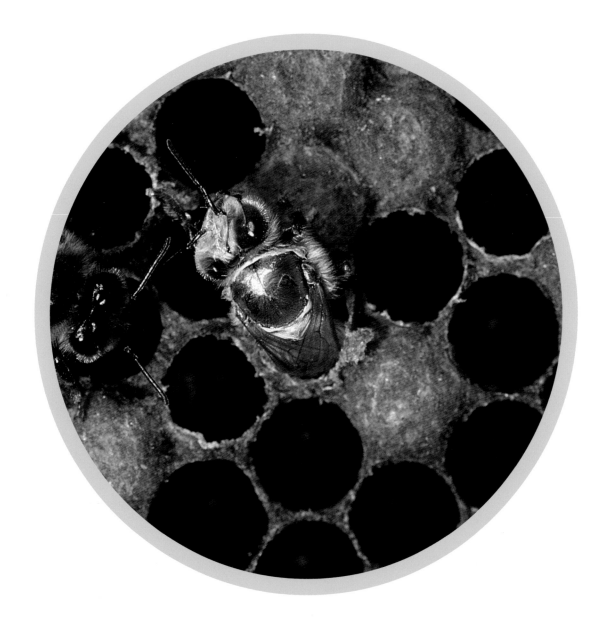

It chews its way through the cap and struggles out of the **cell**, leaving the old pupa case behind. At first, the bee's body is soft, and its wings are crumpled. After a day, its body hardens and it can fly.

The bee leaves the hive.

The new **worker bee** has a job to do. In the summer, worker bees live only about six weeks. For the first two weeks, the bee will work in the **hive** cleaning out the **cells** and looking after the queen and the **drones**.

When it is about three or four weeks old, the bee will leave the hive to find **pollen** and **nectar** in flowers. Other bees tell it where to go by dancing in front of it.

The bee finds food.

Bees are busy among the flowers on warm, sunny days. Flying from plant to plant uses up a lot of energy, so the **worker bee** feeds on **honey** before it leaves the **hive**.

The worker bee collects **pollen** and **nectar** from flowers for the hive. It also takes pollen from one flower to another. This pollinates the flower so it can form seeds.

The bee stores the food.

The bee keeps the **nectar** it collects in a special stomach. When its **honey** stomach is full, it returns home and gives the nectar and the **pollen** to the **house bees**.

The house bees then chew the nectar and turn it into honey. They store the new honey and fresh pollen in empty **honeycomb cells**. When a cell is full, they seal it with wax.

The workers feed the queen.

The workers feed the **queen bee** all the time so that she can continue to lay eggs. She lives only about two or three years. As she gets older, she lays fewer eggs. When this happens, the **hive** workers select a **larva** and feed it extra **royal jelly**. This larva will become the hive's next queen.

Word bank

Cells - where the queen bee places eggs after they are laid. It is a safe environment for them to hatch and grow.

Drones - male bees that are raised and fed by worker bees.

Glands - parts of animals' bodies that produce a substance. Worker bees have glands that produce wax.

Hives - bees' homes or nests. People may keep bees in hives so that they can collect the honey. In the wild, bees often live in hollow trees.

Honey - a sweet, liquidy food produced by bees from the nectar of flowers.

Honeycomb - a collection of wax cells formed by bees. They are used to store honey and raise young bees.

House bees - young worker bees who look after the hive, take care of the queen, and feed the larvae.

Larva - the form a bee takes after it hatches but before it grows skin and wings. Larvae is the plural form of larva.

Nectar - a sweet, sugary liquid that attracts bees to flowers. Bees make honey from nectar.

Pollen - a fine, yellow powder that is produced by male flowers.

Pupa - the stage a bee or other insect goes through as it changes from larva to adult.

Queen bee - the only bee in the hive that lays eggs.

Royal jelly - a rich, liquid food that worker bees feed to larvae.

Worker bees - bees that produce wax, look after the hive, and collect food to feed the larvae.

Life cycle

The queen lays each
egg in a different cell of
the honeycomb.

When it is three or four
weeks old, the bee leaves
the hive to find food.

As soon as the
egg is laid, a bee
larva begins
growing inside it.

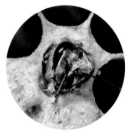

After nine days, the pupa
changes color. It has
turned into an adult.

After three days, the
egg hatches and a bee
larva crawls out.

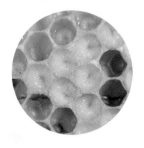

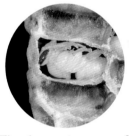

The larva cannot feed
anymore and starts to
change into a pupa.

As the larva grows, it
sheds its skin five
different times.

Eight days after
hatching, the
bee larva is
fully grown.

Index

bee dances 23

cells 6, 7, 8, 9, 16, 17, 18, 21, 22
colonies 4

drones 6, 7, 22

eggs 6, 7, 8, 9, 10, 29

food 11, 14, 15, 17, 18, 24, 25, 26, 27

hives 5, 7, 12, 13, 22, 23, 24, 25
honey 5, 14, 26, 27
honey stomach 26
honeycomb 6, 7, 26, 27
house bees 12, 13

larva *or* larvae 9, 10, 11, 12, 13, 14, 15, 16, 17, 18, 29

nectar 23, 25, 26, 27

pollen 14, 23, 25, 26, 27
pupa 18, 19, 20, 21

queen bees 6, 7, 8, 9, 22, 29

royal jelly 11, 14, 29

wax 16, 17, 20, 21, 26, 27
wings 6, 7, 18, 19
worker bees 6, 7, 10, 12, 14, 16, 18, 28